Courage
PRANAY

BUDDHA
WISDOM LIBRARY

Published by

FiNGERPRINT!
Prakash Books

Fingerprint Publishing
@FingerprintP
@fingerprintpublishingbooks
www.fingerprintpublishing.com

ISBN: 978 93 6214 028 9

Remembering our Buddha-nature
makes us courageous.

**OM MUNI MUNI
MAHAMUNI SHAKYAMUNIYE
SVAHA**

*Imbibing and repeating the Shakyamuni
Buddha Mantra helps us connect with
the Buddha's insight, wisdom, grace,
power, and courage.*

Contents

CHAPTER 1

The Buddha's Vision and Path of Courage

Nothing outside of yourself can ever enable you to get better, stronger/more courageous, richer, quicker, or smarter. Everything is within. Seek nothing outside of yourself.

Miyamoto Musashi,
The Great Samurai Warrior
and Zen Poet-Mystic

In the Buddha's vision, our journey toward self-realization and enlightenment needs the greatest courage. And gathering courage requires us to first *grasp reality as it is,* without distorting our mind with various concepts and conditioned beliefs. By understanding reality as it is, we become ready to face things no matter what, and that is the state of courage! This correlation between perceiving reality with utmost clarity, and living courageously, is one of the Buddha's great gifts to humankind. His path allows us to live in a manner that is brave, truthful, rooted and strong.

Ultimately, the measure of courage in the Buddhist vision is how we move toward our state of grasping our own Buddha-nature and realizing how we are comprised of that ultimate Buddha quality that exists within all beings.

The Buddha, in his own life, exemplifies the most profound valor, clarity, and depth of courage. It was his sheer thirst for truth, and his infinite courage, which propelled him unto the mystic path.

In the Buddha's vision, the idea of courage, or *viriya,* is one within which we have noble fortitude, perseverance, and determination. That way, we can get over all challenges in life, surpass all obstacles, and attain the utmost bliss, enlightenment, liberation, and so on.

On his path, the Buddha had to face significant obstacles. He had people who were opposed to him, such as his disciple Devadatta, who tried to kill him. Yet, the Buddha persevered in his graceful, noble courage without having any malevolence toward those who sought to harm him. And that is the way of the Bodhisattvas and the Arhats (as the knowers of enlightenment are respectively called in Mahayana Buddhism and Theravada Buddhism).

Buddha walked on, no matter what! He used to use a phrase, 'Charaiveti-Charaiveti, which means that one just needs to keep walking on, no matter what! And that is what he exemplified in his own life. On his road to enlightenment, it is said that the evil force called Mara tried to tempt him and tried to put obstacles on his way to enlightenment. Yet, he overcame all these obstacles and temptations, going beyond the delusion, leading to utmost clarity about our multiverse, cosmos, universe, consciousness, etc.

In the Buddhist language, true courage means determining ourselves to transcend the cycle of *samsara*, which is the cycle of birth, death, and rebirth. Hence, we must take courage from Buddha's teachings.

His teachings are profound and practical. For example, Buddhism says that we should not fear Mara—the idea of the tempter, the obstacle maker—because it emanates our mind and limitations. If we overcome our minds' obstacles, we attain virtue, wisdom, and compassion, moving beyond ignorance and fear.

And truly, when we move beyond fear, we can achieve all things.

Courage is the very foundation upon which Gautam's Buddha's whole path is about. And again, in the Buddha's way of courage, it is not about reckless bravado. It is about the fearlessness of confronting our limitations, attachments, and desires. That way, we can realize the truth of ultimate reality and the truth of ourselves.

Over the millennia, countless individuals have embraced Gautam Buddha's message of inner courage. Alexander was deeply moved by the Buddha's message. The samurai warriors of medieval Japan, the embodiment of courage, imbibed Buddha's message and put it into the Zen code of Bushido, which combines the warrior spirit with the poet's mystic spirit in the quest for enlightenment.

The greatest samurai, Miyamoto Musashi, encapsulated the principles of courage in his famous book, *The Book of Five Rings*. But he did not stop at the virtue of courage. He made courage the very path we must walk if we are to attain the ultimate Buddha virtues, which are kindness, compassion, nobility, grace, etc.

The Buddha's courage inspires us to let go of our ego-driven desires and our selfish attachments. It enables us to recognize the interconnectedness of our entire existence and realize that interconnectedness with the ultimate truth within ourselves. On the one hand, the Buddha inspired individuals to muster courage to transcend the cycle of suffering. And on the other hand, he inspired people to move toward enlightenment. He also told us to have such guts in life that we strive tirelessly for the welfare and liberation of others.

The courage of the Buddhas is encapsulated in an anecdote: The Buddha awaits at the gates of enlightenment for the last being in this multiverse to enter the portals of enlightenment—and only then will He Himself enter those portals! That is the ideal of enlightenment.

When we embrace Buddha's teachings and the nobility of courage, we begin holding the master key to unlock our profound spiritual and material potential for value creation.

Buddhism amalgamates personal enlightenment and compassionate action, spurred on by the courage to create a world where we can be true value-creators. Hence, imbuing the Buddha's message of courage into our own lives is not only beneficial for our own spiritual journey but also contributes positively to the well-being of the entire world!

Om Vajrayogini Hum Phat Svaha
Om Vajra Heruka Hum Phat Svaha
(Mystic mantras that awaken
nobility and courage)

CHAPTER 2

A Powerful Practice to Awaken Courage

A prayerful meditation to awaken courage is to simply repeat and internalize these words within yourself: "Buddho, Buddho, Buddho." Known as the practice of Buddhanusati or reflection upon the Buddha, this meditation is means to recollect the qualities of the Buddha—especially those of noble courage, compassion, and inspired wisdom. It is a powerful tool to remind us of us to need to be noble, courageous, meditative, and strong! Internalizing this mantra and using it can instantly awaken our best, bravest, and strongest qualities.

This invocation or mantra guides us to reflect on the profound qualities of the Buddha, which in turn empowers us with courage while cultivating deep peace and calmness within. We can—and should—easily incorporate this invocation into our prayer or meditation practice to experience its transformative effects.

Contemplating the Buddha awakens fearlessness and wisdom, connecting us with our inner Buddha-nature inherent within. By focusing on this simple mantra, we quiet the mind and deepen our connection to the truth of existence, liberating ourselves from fear, ignorance, agitation, and anxiety.

Om Ah Hum Vajra Guru Pema Siddhi Hum
(Mantric invocation to Guru Padmasambhava,
invoking blessings for spiritual realisation
and courageous, enlightened living)

CHAPTER 3

Mystic Teachings on Courage

*Cut the mind at its root,
and rest in naked awareness.*

Tilopa, the Master of
Mahamudra Buddhism

The mystic teachings of the Buddha illuminate the path to living with purity, strength of mind, and courage. They guide us toward embracing the noble path and attaining a state of inner nobility and bravery.

Central to this journey are the "10 Profound States of Mind" that Buddhism encourages us to cultivate. These states are *truthfulness, flexibility, capability, control, peacefulness, pure goodness, non-defilement, non-attachment, broad-mindedness, and magnanimity*—all of which empower us to embody fearlessness and inner strength.

By anchoring our minds in these profound states, we naturally become stronger, more energetic, and more dynamic in our approach to life.

Furthermore, Buddhism emphasizes the Eightfold Noble Path, a foundational teaching of Gautam Buddha, which emphasizes *correctness in views, thoughts, speech, conduct, livelihood, effort, mindfulness, and meditation*. Following this path leads to immense strength and bravery within ourselves.

In addition, Buddhism teaches us the "Profound Applications of the Mind," which, if cultivated, lead to an invigorated state of being free from fear. These applications are *purity, stability, relinquishment, freedom from craving, non-regression, firmness, and glowing brightness*. These qualities of mind enable us to face life's challenges with courage, resilience, and fortitude.

By adhering to the principles of the Eightfold Noble Path and nurturing the profound states of mind and its applications, we become deeply fortified and courageous within ourselves, fearlessly navigating the complexities of life with grace and wisdom.

Additionally, Buddhism imparts fundamental rules for ethical living, known as the Dasa Kushala. These guidelines include refraining from acts such as killing, stealing, committing adultery, telling lies, using harsh words, causing enmity between people, engaging in idle gossip, and fostering non-greediness, non-anger, and avoidance of wrong views. Adhering to these principles is essential for living fearlessly and wisely.

Moreover, Buddhism identifies ten fetters, or *Samyojana*, that hinder our ability to live fearlessly. These fetters include beliefs in individuality, skepticism, attachment to rituals, excessive craving or desire, hatred, pride, over-excitability, and ignorant behavior. Overcoming these behaviors is crucial for cultivating courage and wisdom in our lives.

Furthermore, the Buddhist scriptures introduce 'Ten Contemplations' or meditations, known as *Anusatti*, which awaken courage within us. These meditations encompass *meditating upon (contemplating) various things, specifically* the Enlightened One (Buddha), the teachings of the Dharma, the Buddhist community (*Sangha*), discipline (*Sheela*), generosity (*Dana*), deities (*Deva*), death*, the body, concentration on the breath (*Anapanasati*), and peace (*Santi*). These contemplations serve as powerful tools for overcoming fear and fostering courage within us.

Besides these mystic teachings, Buddhism offers '10 Guiding Principles for Living', designed to lead us toward a noble existence characterized by fearlessness and clarity of mind. These rules serve as pillars for cultivating virtues and inner strength:

---

* Notably, the contemplation on death holds particular significance in Japanese Buddhism, echoing the practices of paths like the Samurai. By meditating upon death, individuals aim to overcome all fears and awaken courage within themselves. Buddha himself even prescribed this meditation to novices who joined his Sangha, encouraging them to spend time in cemeteries witnessing the impermanence of life. Additionally, practices such as contemplation on the body and concentration on the breath (Anapanasati) further aid in cultivating courage and inner peace.

1. **Association with Virtuous Individuals:** Cultivate relationships with virtuous people while avoiding those who lack moral integrity.

2. **Creating a Conducive Environment:** Reside in surroundings conducive to spiritual practice and character development.

3. **Engagement in Spiritual Learning:** Dedicate time to learning about mysticism, Buddhism, and spirituality and focusing on personal growth and development.

4. **Family Responsibilities:** Fulfill responsibilities toward parents, spouse, children, and family, nurturing harmonious relationships.

5. **Generosity and Sharing:** Share time, energy, resources, and joy with others, fostering genuine goodwill and inner strength.

6. **Cultivation of Virtue:** Uphold virtuous conduct, abstaining from intoxicants, gambling, and other harmful behaviors.

7. **Humility, Gratitude, and Simplicity:** Embrace humility, gratitude, and a simple way of life. These practices purify the inner self and foster clarity of mind. Even renowned figures like Steve Jobs advocated

for simplicity, aligning with the principles of Zen Buddhism.

8. **Seeking Wise Company:** Surround yourself with learned individuals who possess the wisdom of the Buddha's teachings, providing guidance and inspiration.

9. **Alignment with the Four Noble Truths:** Base your life on understanding the Four Noble Truths, which elucidate the nature of suffering and the path to its transcendence.

10. **Integration of Meditation and Contemplation:** Make life a meditative and contemplative practice, deepening awareness and insight.

Embracing these principles empowers us to navigate life with clarity, strength, and wisdom, fostering inner resilience and spiritual growth.

Budu Saranai

May the blessings of the Buddha be with you.

Teruwan Saranai

May the blessings of the Buddha,
Dhamma and Sangha be with you.

(Sacred Greetings from
Sinhalese Buddhism)

CHAPTER 4

The Buddha's Way of Courage: Five Key Insights

Running after thoughts, you become
like the dog chasing a thrown stick!
Be like the lion: do not chase the stick,
instead turn toward the thrower!

Milarepa, the Great
Tibetan Yogi

AUTHENTICITY AND COURAGE

In Buddhism, authentic courage is discovered through embracing one's true self or Buddha-nature. This journey involves deep introspection, contemplation, and meditation—a courageous exploration that imbues significance into every act.

Turning inward and embarking on the path of self-discovery, one taps into an inherent wellspring of courage. This inner strength renders life's trials powerless against the newfound fortitude.

ADAPTING WITH COURAGE

From the Buddhist perspective, genuine courage lies in recognizing the inherent impermanence of existence. It requires acknowledging life's ever-changing nature and embracing adaptability across the realms of mind, heart, and body.

A sincere Buddhist practitioner remains open to adaptation, drawing inspiration from Gautam Buddha's transformative journey into monkhood. In the Buddhist tradition, courage springs from embracing life's continual evolution.

CULTIVATING STEADFAST COURAGE

Buddhist teachings emphasize that courage stems from embracing all experiences as invaluable lessons. This fosters unwavering and steadfast courage, essential for navigating life's challenges and victories.

Viewing every life event as an opportunity for personal growth cultivates a resilient and enduring courage. This fearlessness remains unwavering amidst life's fluctuations.

EMBRACING UNCERTAINTY: THE NOBLE PATH OF WISDOM

In Buddhism, embodied by Sakyamuni Gautam Buddha, true courage transcends the need for absolute certainty. Gautam Buddha's nobility emanates from his humility and gentle nature—he embraced uncertainty without claiming omniscience.

Acknowledging our limitations is a courageous step that leads to deeper understanding and the discovery of truth. True fearlessness emerges when one embraces uncertainty, facilitating the profound exploration of existential truths.

LIBERATION

Gautam Buddha envisioned liberation from rigid belief systems at the heart of Buddhism. He aimed to liberate individuals from the confines of faith-based dogmas, guiding them toward meditative awareness.

Refusing belief systems demands courage, challenging individuals to cultivate an open mind and heart. Thus, Buddhism is a profoundly courageous philosophy, encouraging individuals to rely on their own reason and common sense.

In the words of Buddha: "Believe nothing, no matter where you read it or who said it, unless it agrees with your own reason and common sense."

CHAPTER 5

Seven Steps to Courageous Living

1. EMBRACING ALONENESS: FINDING COURAGE IN SOLITUDE

Buddhism teaches us to cultivate contentment within ourselves, challenging the fear of loneliness that often arises in solitude. True courage, according to Buddhist philosophy, lies in not avoiding aloneness by constantly seeking external company or distractions.

While social connections and familial support are valuable, genuine fulfillment and courage emerge when one finds joy, bliss, and contentment in solitude. It is about transcending the need for constant external stimuli and discovering the strength to be content even when alone.

2. BUDDHISM'S EMPOWERING MESSAGE: THE PATH TO ENLIGHTENMENT WITHIN

At the core of Buddhism lies the empowering message that enlightenment is attainable for all. Gautam Buddha emphasized the inherent equality between himself and others, asserting that anyone can achieve enlightenment through self-belief, conviction, and courage.

This internalized belief forms the foundation of Buddhist courage—an unwavering confidence in the innate Buddha nature within every individual. From this wellspring of inner courage, all other forms of bravery derive their strength.

3. THE COURAGE
OF RENUNCIATION

In Buddhism, true courage manifests in the ability to renounce worldly attachments. Gautam Buddha's life exemplified this spirit of renunciation—he relinquished his royal life, palace, and kingdom to pursue a higher calling.

Renunciation, the act of letting go of anger, jealousy, greed, and attachment to thoughts, is a profound test of courage. This concept, echoed in Zen Buddhism, emphasizes the necessity of sacrifice to achieve excellence in life.

4. COURAGE IN THE
PURSUIT OF TRUTH

Genuine courage in Buddhism is embodied by those who relentlessly pursue truth, willing to relinquish everything in their quest. Truth and courage are intertwined, as true courage thrives only in the support of truth.

Those aligned with truth draw courage from standing on its side, championing noble causes, triumphing over falsehood. Genuine courage shines brightest in the pursuit of truth.

5. THE SAMURAI'S CODE
OF NOBLE COURAGE

Living by the samurai code of Bushido, inspired by Zen Buddhism, exemplifies a spirit of dignified bravery. Unwavering and uncompromising, the noble warrior fights for justice with joy and courage, embodying Buddhist principles of righteous action.

Maintaining an unwavering stance on justice and rightness, whether as a warrior or in any role, embodies the essence of Buddhist wisdom. This dignified courage not only grows within oneself but also inspires others.

6. ZEN CLARITY AND COURAGE

In Zen Buddhism, true courage lies in perceiving reality without the distortions of the conditioned mind. Masters like Bodhidharma emphasize clear perception, free from personal biases and preferences—an approach known as naked awareness.

This courageous perception allows one to exist and perceive reality as it is, unclouded by the mind's conditioning. From this clear perception, all other forms of courage in life naturally emerge, rooted in an authentic understanding of reality.

7. SELF-WORTH

One of Gautam Buddha's most significant contributions was instilling awareness of their inherent worth in people. He emphasized that every individual possesses a divine intuition and Buddha nature, making them immensely worthy, regardless of their life's position or individual capacity. Remembering this innate worthiness, as highlighted by Gautam Buddha, is a constant source of encouragement, preventing feelings of despair. According to Buddha's teachings, true courage stems from a sense of self-worth. Nurture this courage, it is crucial not to let others undermine your self-worth by being swayed by their opinions. The essence of Buddhism lies in following your light and recognizing your intrinsic value.

CHAPTER 6

Indian and Japanese Prayers for Courage

The 'Buddham Sharanam Gacchami' prayer is one of the ancient most Buddhist prayers. It is in the ancient language of the Buddha, which is Pali. It goes like this:

Buddham Sharanam Gacchami,
Dhammam Sharanam Gacchami,
Sangham Sharanam Gacchami.

This means *I take refuge in the Buddha; I take refuge in the Dhamma, I take refuge in the Sangha* or commune.

Invoking such refuge within the Buddha, his Dhamma, and his Sangha creates an umbrella of protection around us. It helps allay our fears and leads us to fearlessness.

Another ancient veneration or prayer in Pali goes like this:

Namo tassa bhagavato arahato
samma sambuddhassa

This means *Homage to the blessed one, the worthy one, the fully enlightened one. I take refuge in the Buddha, the Dhamma, and the Sangha until I attain enlightenment. By the merit of my practice and the mystic power, may all beings be liberated from suffering and find true peace.*

Apart from ancient Indian Buddhist prayers in Pali, there are several prayers in Japanese Buddhism which imbue us with graceful strength and courage. For example, the Samurai Prayer for Courage is famously included in the book on the mystic-martial text, the Hagakure. The Hagakure is the most practical and spiritual guide for the Samurai and was written by Yamamoto Tsunetomo. The prayer goes like this: "In the words of the ancients, one should make his decision within seven breaths. It is a matter of being determined and having the spirit to break through to the other side!"

This teaching in the Hagakure contains the secret of fearlessness and that we should be decisive and bold in our lives. That takes away fear and enables us to act with utmost courage. The prayer tells us about the value of determination—determination can help us make real breakthroughs! When we have decisiveness and determination, we can face up to anything in the world. Then, automatically, the courage in us becomes pooled and becomes strong. We become swift in our actions, fearless in our thoughts, and so on.

Another Japanese phrase inspired by the spirit of Buddhism is *'Ganbatte Kudasai.'* This phrase implies 'Do your best,' ' Hang in there' or 'Make your best effort.' This phrase in Japanese motivates us and others to have a spirit of fearlessness and determination, perseverance! It arouses us to continue with great courage in whatever one does—no matter what the odds against one!

In a way, this phrase summarizes the very spirit of Japan and the Japanese people! Which is about acting with fearlessness and perseverance, no matter what (as evidenced by the stellar Japanese response to critical events such as Tsunamis and earthquakes). We must imbibe this courageous, persevering, determined spirit in life, whether in inter-personal other areas such as interpersonal work we pursue or other areas such as interpersonal relationships. This phrase is a lovely way to inspire others and inspire oneself.

CHAPTER 7

Root Means to Courageous Living

The various paths of Buddhism prescribe certain root means to unlock our capability for courageous and virtuous living. For example, the Rinzai Zen in Japanese Buddhism tells us that we implement the 'Three Necessities,' which are:

1. Having great faith
2. Having great doubt, that is, being able to question our conditioned beliefs about reality
3. Having a strong will, such that it overpowers all challenging circumstances and helps us move forward.

Moreover, the Buddhist teachings of Pai Chang (the Zen master) teach us the 'Three Fundamentals,' which are:
1. To be detached from everything
2. To not remain abiding in detachment but to be able to move on from a state of detachment
3. Non-understanding of non-abiding: This means going beyond intellectual concepts of abiding or non-abiding and finding direct insight into reality - through self-understanding and understanding of universal truth.

Moreover, in the Buddhist scriptures, we are told to apply 'Four Mindfulnesses', these being:
1. Mindfulness of the body
2. Mindfulness of feelings
3. Mindfulness of thoughts
4. Mindfulness of all things

What we should avoid on the path to dynamic and courageous living are called the 'Three Unwholesome Roots' in Buddhism, which are:

1. Desire
2. Hatred
3. Delusion

Furthermore, Buddhism teaches us the very dynamic concept of the 'Three Stages on the Path of Purification,' these being:

1. Moral conduct and character, i.e., Shila
2. Mental concentration, i.e., Samadhi
3. Liberating knowledge of human existence, i.e., Panna.

CHAPTER 8

Spiritual Purification and Dhamma

According to Buddhism, the essence of fearless and courageous living lies in spiritual purification. We naturally embody courage, contentment, and boundless energy when we attain spiritual purity. This process, known as *Dhutanga* in Buddhist texts, involves shedding all negative aspects from within us.

Through *Dhutanga*, we cultivate strength, fulfillment, discipline, and moderation, leading to lives marked by excellence and courage.

Simplicity is at the heart of spiritual purification, as advocated in the ancient Pali texts of Buddhism. Simplifying our lives allows for the natural emergence of purification. Zen Buddhism emphasizes the practicality of simple living, as exemplified by individuals like Steve Jobs, who found courage and clarity through meditation and adherence to Buddhist principles. The Buddha embodied simplicity, advising his followers to be content and satisfied. True simplicity empowers us from within and enables us to face life's challenges without fear.

In Buddhism, afflictions such as old age, disease, and death are seen as divine messengers, urging us to confront the deeper questions of life and emerge stronger and more courageous. Contemplating the inevitability of human limitations, as the Buddha encourages, fosters inner strength and resilience. This process leads us to embrace the Four Noble Truths, which encapsulate the nature of suffering, its origin, cessation, and the path to liberation.

Dhamma, the teachings of the Buddha, serves as the path to courage and enlightenment. It encompasses doctrines and principles that guide us toward good conduct, wisdom, contentment, and inner strength. Embracing Dhamma as a way of life is the key to realizing true courage and attaining enlightenment.

CHAPTER 9

The Buddha's Words for Courageous and Dynamic Living

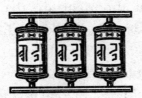

Various scriptures, such as the Dhammapada and other Buddhist texts, give us an idea of what it truly means to imbibe values for courageous and dynamic living.

The Dhammapada itself is very key to the Pali canon of Buddhism. It tells us how our thoughts and actions shape our way of living. Other Buddhist scriptures that teach us these things are the Lotus Sutra from Mahayana Buddhism, which talks about how to use skilful means and meditation for enlightenment, considered universal. The Lotus Sutra tells us that the seed of potential for Buddhahood exists within all. The Diamond Sutra of Mahayana Buddhism tells us that our perception of reality is illusory; hence, we must transcend all attachments.

Though short, the Heart Sutra from Mahayana Buddhism is an important text that teaches us the emptiness of existence. While the *Tao Te Ching* from Taoism is not really Buddhist, it has some very Buddhist qualities within it and is considered in Zen Buddhism to be a pivotal text for dynamic and courageous living. It tells us about the way or the Tao and how to implement simplicity in life to live fearlessly, dynamically and in an enlightened way.

Digging deep into the Buddhist texts, we come to the core teachings of the Buddha which teach us in many ways how to live without any fear in our hearts. The Buddha says, 'All conditioned things are impermanent,' and,' and through this teaching, he tells us that all things are subject to change. Hence, we must cultivate calmness within us and transcend our fixation and attachment on things that come and go. This attitude creates dynamism.

Moreover, the Buddha says, 'What we think that we become.' This teaching tells us how we must shape our thoughts to be positive, compassionate, and dynamic. In other words, we must create a wholeness of thoughts and emotions within us to live courageously.

The Buddha, in his teaching on the Four Noble Truths, also tells us that life is suffering. Through this teaching, we understand that it is only through the transcendence of suffering, through the quest for Buddhahood, that we can attain true happiness, joy, and fearlessness in life. Suffering can be a great impetus to find a higher truth. It teaches us to come face to face with reality and thereby transcend it.

The Buddha says, 'Do not seek for peace from the outside. Remember that peace comes from within you.' This teaching of the Buddha tells us that our state of being is about how we are in our internal state and that our inner state of being determines our dynamism, fearlessness, happiness, and peace in life. If we truly seek dynamism and fearlessness, we should not rely on the material world. We must cultivate these things as inner qualities.

Further, the Buddha tells us about the Eightfold Noble Path, which comprises the interconnected principles of *right views, right intentions, right speech, right action, right livelihood, right effort, right mindfulness, and right concentration*. This Eightfold Path helps make us strong, mindful, compassionate, and wise within ourselves. The Eightfold Path is a sound basis for our psycho-spiritual development, and following it keeps us balanced and dynamic.

Overall, the Buddha's teachings help us discover ourselves and live lives that are truly fearless. He teaches us to cultivate courage in the face of adversity. In a world filled with uncertainty and challenges, courage is a quality that enables individuals to face adversity with strength, resilience, and determination. The timeless teachings of the Buddha offer profound insights into the nature of courage and guide how to cultivate it in our lives.

Siddhartha Gautam, known as the Buddha, exemplified courage in his pursuit of enlightenment. He left behind a legacy of wisdom that inspires countless individuals seeking inner strength and bravery. At the heart of the Buddha's teachings is the recognition of suffering (*dukkha*) as an inherent aspect of human existence. However, he also emphasized that suffering arises from attachment and craving, which can be transcended through the cessation of desire and the cultivation of wisdom and compassion. This forms the foundation of the Four Noble Truths (described above), which outline the nature of suffering, its causes, its cessation, and the path to its cessation. The path prescribed by the Buddha offers practical guidance on how to live a life of courage and inner strength.

By cultivating Buddha's teaching qualities in daily life, individuals can align themselves with the path of awakening and find the courage to confront life›s challenges with grace and fortitude. Mindfulness and meditation are central Buddhist practices, offering powerful tools for cultivating courage and resilience. Mindfulness means pure awareness, bringing us face-to-face with our feelings and emotions—in a balanced, calm and clear manner.

CHAPTER 10

Unbinding Fear: The Liberating Wisdom of Buddhist Scriptures

In Buddhism, the concept of *Gantha*, or bindings/ties, serves as a roadmap to break free from delusion and live fearlessly.

The *things that bind us or tie us down* include ill-will (*vyapada*), covetousness (*abhijja*), fanaticism (*idamsaccàbhinivesa*) and over-attachment to rules and rituals (*shilabbata-paràmàsa*). All these factors restrict spiritual growth and lead to stagnation.

Covetousness binds us to material possessions, while hostility toward others traps us in negative emotions. Overemphasis on rules and rituals stifles dynamism, while fanaticism hinders true insight into existence.

By transcending these bindings or ties and gaining insight into our nature, we unlock our potential for boundless freedom, fearlessness, and enlightenment. Embracing such wisdom, we are to embark on a path of dynamic living and the fearless exploration of life's mysteries.

FEARLESSNESS THROUGH MINDFULNESS

In Buddhism, cultivating courage involves breaking free from the cycle of negative thoughts and emotions, known as *Domannasa* or sad-mindedness. This state often arises from harboring hatred and grudges toward others, leading to a perpetuation of sorrow and pessimism. Individuals can achieve emotional balance and fearlessness by refraining from indulging in sorrow and recognizing its role in fostering negativity.

Central to Buddhist teachings is the concept of Dukkha, which is the inherent sorrow of life. This concept underscores the need for mindfulness and acceptance of life's transient nature. Understanding Dukkha as the first of the Four Noble Truths enables one to navigate life fearlessly, transcending the hold of pleasure and pain.

Through insight meditation or Vipassana, practitioners are to attain profound insight into the impermanent nature of existence, paving the way for liberation from fear, suffering, and so on . . .

CHAPTER 11

Buddhist Keys for Dynamic Living

Buddhism offers clear-cut laws and keys for living dynamically in an awakened and enlightened state. Particularly, it describes the 'Seven Factors of Enlightenment' or the 'Limbs of Awakening,' each serving as a pathway to living courageously and dynamically. These factors are known as the *sapta bodhyanga* in

Indian Buddhism, the *byang chub yan lag* in Tibetan Buddhism, and the *juezhi* or *putifen* in Chinese Buddhism. The factors or limbs of awakened living are:

1. Mindfulness, or *Smriti*
2. Investigation of Truth, or *Dharmapravacaya*
3. Determination and Energetic Perseverance, called *Virya*
4. Blissfulness, Joy, and Rapture, called *Priti*
5. Calmness and Tranquility, called *Prashrabdhi*
6. Focus and Concentration, called *Samadhi*
7. Equanimity, or *Upeksha*

Being mindful of these seven factors spontaneously enables us to live courageously and openly with a spirit of great determination.

Conversely, Buddhism also teaches us to avoid certain behaviors if we are to live dynamically. These are encapsulated as the 'Ten 'Fetters' or the Samyojana:

1. The view of an enduring self, or Satkaya Drishti. Believing in the immortality of the self impedes present-moment dynamism.
2. Over-attachment to dogmatic rules, rituals, and so on, known as Shila Vrata Paramarsha.

3. Excessive doubt, called Vichikitsa, hinders fearless living and leads to delusion.

4. Overwhelming craving for sensual gratification, or Kamachanda, confines us to limited existence.

5. Malice, envy, jealousy, and similar traits, known as Vyapada, keep us small-minded and preoccupied with others rather than focusing on our evolution.

6. Obsession with materiality, called Rupa Raga.

7. Excessive craving for the immaterial realm, known as Arupya Raga.

8. Pride and conceit, referred to as Mana.

9. Delusion, termed Moha.

10. Restlessness and excessive worry, called *Audhatya*, obstructs the inner stillness necessary for dynamic and courageous living.

By considering these key aspects of Buddhism and aligning with its teachings on the correct approach to life, we can live far more bravely—with greater inner strength and energy.

CHAPTER 12

The Courage to Be Yourself

FREEDOM OF INDIVIDUAL CHOICE IN BUDDHISM

Buddhism emphasizes the profound idea that genuine character emerges from personal choice. Individuality and true personality are products of one's personal search, not predetermined by birth into a specific religion, nationality, or cultural background. The truly spiritual seeker in Buddhism nurtures the nobility of nature through their own free will, not merely conforming to external factors.

The revolutionary aspect of Buddhism lies in its rejection of the claim, made by many world religions that individuals are born into a particular faith and must adhere to it. Instead, Buddhism encourages the pursuit of truth emerging from the heart, leading to a transformative journey where individuals create their reality. The path involves moving toward one's unique individuality, representing the most noble part of Buddhism.

Gautam Buddha's teachings highlight the futility of living according to past conditionings, which create illusions and move individuals away from truth. Being shaped by the collective mind prevents the realization of one's individual self. Buddha advocates for the beautiful and creative choice of one's path, emphasizing the role of a true seeker over merely being labeled as a Buddhist. The true seeker, possessing the quality of authenticity, is the only requirement on the path of Buddhism.

Buddhism is portrayed as a unique journey, beginning a real pilgrimage where external influences do not predetermine the destination. Unlike ordinary pilgrimages, where an outward predetermined destination decides the desired destination, the true path of the Buddhist seeker involves creating one's destination—a movement toward personal freedom, potential realization, and the peaks of consciousness.

In its revolutionary and sophisticated nature, Buddhism avoids being occupied with the status quo and conditioned beliefs. Instead, it encourages individuals to discover the poetry and music of the self in the innermost core, free from external dictates. We are living under external dictators, whether religion, nationality, or social position, is discouraged by Buddha. The call is to reject man-given tags and recognize the higher and nobler self within—embracing the true essence of individuality and freedom.

UNVEILING THE BUDDHA WITHIN: A REVOLUTIONARY UNDERSTANDING

According to Buddhist philosophy, life is an unveiling of the enlightened being, the Buddha, within oneself. The process involves tearing off layers of conditioned thoughts and personalities imposed by external influences. At the core, what remains is the authentic self, which has the potential to reach the highest states of being.

Buddhism challenges the ordinary way of living dictated by others' thoughts, traditions, and cultures. Pursuing joy and realizing one's real and original self-energy require breaking free from conditioned habits and practices. True individuals in creativity and intuitive seeking go beyond societal dictates, recognizing themselves as original parts of existence rather than second-hand labels imposed by religion or nationality.

Buddha's revolutionary insight emphasizes that individuals should not be distorted or disfigured by external influences, including education and societal conditioning, during their formative years. Instead, one should be shaped by the inner journey of self-discovery—a pinnacle of life. This perspective holds practical value, particularly for those aspiring to be innovators or leaders who break away from the collective evolution dictated by society.

True leaders considered pathfinders or pathbreakers, allow their inner evolution to unfold from their interior selves. They reject the notion of collective evolution, refusing to live according to societal dictates. True leadership involves creating one's path, even if it means cutting through the rock of conditioning. By eliminating conditioned responses, tensions dissolve automatically.

Conditioning, which brings concomitant tensions due to societal expectations, can be mitigated by cultivating a sense of detachment. Detachment, a significant aspect of Buddhist spiritual philosophy, involves being aloof, cool, and detached from societal judgments and opinions. This detachment allows individuals to realize their higher selves, leading to a consciousness of higher energy and confidence. True confidence is not based on believing what others say but on experiencing one's journey.

As perceived reality sheds away, individuals attain their reality. Observing oneself and moving to the center of one's being, gathering energies within, and becoming a passionate and valuable worker in the world—all these aspects align with the transformative and empowering teachings of Buddhism.

NURTURING ORIGINALITY: THE MAVERICK SPIRIT IN BUDDHISM

Creativity and innovation, essential for progress and new ideas in the world, require individuals with inner confidence who refuse to conform to external dictates. The collective mind often stifles creativity and breakthrough thinking, emphasizing conformity. True breakthroughs occur when individuals embrace their unique wings, flying into unknown skies and fulfilling themselves materially, spiritually, and emotionally. It is crucial not to let others' ideas possess you to the extent that your potential remains dormant.

Everyone carries a seed of potential, yet many settle for living according to societal norms and the status quo. The mavericks are the few who muster the determination to sprout forth as their original selves. While it may require extra effort, it is a worthwhile and natural way to live—a path to a divine life.

The lives of Buddhas, Bodhisattvas, mystics, and great individuals across various fields underscore the importance of originality. Whether in sciences, arts, music, business, or technology, individuals who break away from conventional thinking leave a lasting impact. The practicality of this quality lies in not allowing external influences to dominate. Like Steve Jobs, Mavericks embody individuality as a bedrock of life, shaping the culture of companies like Apple with maverick thinking—away from the crowd and awakened to one's original state.

Being a more valuable person in the world is not about acquired morality but individual choices and motivations. Buddhism encourages individuals to find true morality within their consciousness. Gautam Buddha asserted that anyone acting with consciousness cannot be immoral, as acting with the purest and highest consciousness radiates light, loving truth, cosmic beauty, and empathy. Consequently, one's actions reflect radiance, beauty, and value.

A critical examination of the mind's content reveals that much of it is learned from others and absorbed from society. Move toward the more realistic aspect of one's being and the spontaneity of one's energy, individuals must realize the constant need to transform their lives based on their understanding. This ongoing process leads to profound realizations, offering the energy to cleanse the mind of unnecessary conditioning and move effortlessly toward realizing one's highest energy. This, in turn, manifests in all aspects of life, fostering a more successful and fulfilling existence.

CHAPTER 13

Buddhist Perspectives on Fearless Living

GUTS, BOLDNESS, COURAGEOUS ENERGY (VIRIYA)

The essence of the Buddha's teachings is encapsulated in the call for guts, boldness, and courage, particularly a unique form of spiritual courage. This courage surpasses the ordinary; it is the audacity to relinquish the ego and transcend the limitations of the mind. The path advocated by the Buddha leads into the sphere of divine understanding, which exists beyond all things yet forms the foundation of all existence.

FEELING THE DIVINE
HAND IN EVERYDAY LIFE

The message of boldness emphasizes experiencing the divine in the intricacies of daily life. Often, people do not perceive the hand of the divine in their routine existence, and if they do, it is often confined to the realm of belief systems or religious affiliations. The Buddha's path encourages the integration of the material and the spiritual in everyday life. By infusing the spiritual into the material, one can tangibly feel the divine as an integral part of their lived experience, moving beyond mere belief systems.

INTEGRATION OF MATERIAL
AND SPIRITUAL LIFE

The way of the Buddha calls for integrating both practical and spiritual aspects in daily life. This integration is an invitation to infuse the spiritual into every dimension of material existence. Through this, the divine ceases to be an abstract concept and becomes a palpable reality in one's immediate experience. This transformative shift requires the courage to break free from unnecessary shackles and fully participate in the divine essence that permeates the cosmos. Spiritual courage is the freedom to heed the call of the mystical aspect of life and feel unbound within oneself.

ACTIVE PARTICIPATION IN THE PROCESS OF CREATION

Buddhism boldly asserts that individuals are not merely created beings but active participants in the ongoing creation process. It challenges the notion that God is the sole creator while humans are mere creations. Instead, Buddhism posits that individuals are co-participants in the cyclical process of creation and destruction, an infinite cycle without a discernible beginning or end. This continuous process involves the birth and destruction of universes, leading to their rebirth in an eternal cosmic dance.

BUDDHISM AS A TRANSFORMATIVE PROCESS

Buddhism, as described, is a bold and transformative path that challenges the conventional understanding of humanity's role in the cosmos. Unlike the notion of God as the sole creator and humans as passive creations, Buddhism asserts that individuals are active co-participants in the perpetual cycle of creation and destruction. This continuous process, characterized by an infinite cycle without a discernible beginning or end, involves universes' birth, destruction, and rebirth.

DISCONNECTING FROM THE PAST AND EMBRACING NEWNESS

The transformative nature of Buddhism emphasizes the need to disconnect from the past and embrace the perpetual newness of creation. It advocates for a resurrection of the best within individuals. This resurrection process is facilitated by embodying boldness and luminosity in understanding. According to Buddhism, the heart of the mystic search lies in awakening to the newness of creation, disentangling from past conditioning, and allowing the best within oneself to come forth.

BRINGING BOLDNESS
AND COURAGE INTO LIFE

Buddhism encourages individuals to intuitively incorporate elements of boldness and courage into every aspect of life. The fundamental message is to be absorbed by the Buddha, who exemplified determination in his quest. Individuals can feel energized by allowing the spirit of boldness and the courage to do what is right to permeate one's being. This, in turn, enables them to transcend narrow aims and goals, participating in the totality of life in a more peaceful and meaningful manner.

DETERMINATION AS THE
BEDROCK OF ACHIEVEMENT

As highlighted in Buddhism, the bedrock of all great achievements is determination. The Buddha's life exemplifies this determination as he moved swiftly and clearly toward his goal. The primary objective is to move beyond the prison of conditioned thought. The analogy of the arrow of consciousness flying high into the cosmic realm signifies the quest for realizing Nirvana—the ultimate freedom of recognizing oneself as a living, palpable form of ultimate cosmic energy. In the Buddha's context, determination involves a focused and unwavering commitment to the journey of self-realization and the attainment of ultimate freedom.

BUDDHA'S PATH OF WHOLEHEARTED COURAGE

Buddha's way, as described, is characterized by wholehearted courage. It emphasizes celebrating life by inwardly dancing and rejoicing in the present moment. Buddha's motivation was practical, unlike preaching a philosophical system or presenting an imagined explanation of God. He aimed to immerse people in the truthful ecstasy of their consciousness, helping them realize the bliss of universal consciousness. From this realization, individuals could harness their highest energies to touch the very heart of the mystical foundations of life.

PRACTICAL APPROACH AND MAXIMUM INNER FUNCTIONING

Buddha's practical approach encourages individuals to function inwardly to the maximum. The emphasis is on going beyond tenseness and anxiety. The idea is that outer results in life are maximized by maximizing inner functioning. This approach requires the courage to be patient and trusting. Boldness and guts are essential qualities to seek the higher light of realization, to experience the light of knowing. Without these qualities, the potential for divine or cosmic realization remains unrealized.

RADICAL APPROACH TO SCRIPTURES AND PHILOSOPHIES

Buddha's radical perspective led him to advise his disciples to leave behind scriptures and philosophies. He believed that innate experience is crucial for divine or cosmic realization. Scriptures were considered to obscure truly valuable aspects. According to Buddha, the only real scripture is within oneself—the scripture of oneself. Through this inner exploration, individuals can attain illumined energy, making all things possible.

ACHIEVING NIRVANA THROUGH BOLDNESS AND COURAGE

Buddha asserted that only the truly bold and courageous person can achieve Nirvana. It requires moving beyond mere dreams and transforming realization into lived experience. This boldness involves a radical departure from external sources of knowledge and a deep trust in the inner self. By embodying courage and wholehearted commitment to the path, individuals can unfold the profound experiences that Buddha advocated.

TREMENDOUS QUALITIES OF BUDDHAHOOD AND OVERCOMING FEAR

Buddhahood's qualities involve destroying all that is unnecessary, primarily rooted in fear. By eliminating fear, individuals can reveal pure courage—the innate guts of their being. The key is to recognize that everything needed for any endeavor is already present. Gathering that courage enables individuals to approach activities calmly and quietly, fostering a collected, integrated, and centered mind. In this state, the mind can bring positive value and tap into higher potentialities, inviting subtle yet powerful forces into one's life.

THE NOTHINGNESS AND POTENTIAL IN BUDDHISM

Buddhism explains that everything emerges from a deep nothingness, representing a subtle, unexplainable essence beyond the material senses. This nothingness contains the seeds of balance, totality, and the cosmos. Analogously, the seed of a giant oak tree may seem like nothingness, but it holds the entire tree's potential. Similarly, the Buddha suggests that all potential resides in one's purest state of nothingness. By negating the ego, individuals can unleash their inherent potential, allowing the tree of life to blossom with flowers and fruits of their choosing.

CHOOSING TO BE LUMINOUS AND SELF-EVOLUTION

Human beings can choose to be luminous, radiating with the light of their highest being. However, this requires courage and guts. Without these qualities, one may only reflect other people's lives and thoughts, remaining passive. The path of Buddhahood encourages self-luminosity—a state where individuals explode with their energies from within. According to this path, true spiritual evolution arises from internal sources rather than external influences. This self-luminosity enables individuals to shine with their unique light and contribute authentically to the world.

CHAKRAS AS METAPHORICAL CENTERS OF ENERGY

In Buddhism and Hinduism, chakras are considered metaphorical points or centers of energy within the body. While not physically observable, these chakras symbolize the presence of cosmic power originating from subtle nothingness. The concept underscores the mysterious nature of life and consciousness, emphasizing the need to go beyond the ego for true understanding and joy.

THE COURAGE TO KNOW LIFE'S FOUNDATIONS

Buddhism encourages individuals to cultivate the courage to stop believing in the ego, which is a barrier to understanding truth and experiencing joy. The journey to know the subtlest aspects of life's energy requires a leap into the unknown realms of one's being. This demands courage and guts, urging individuals to break free from mental shells—past and future concerns, fearfulness, and anxiety. The Buddha's teachings aimed to guide both ascetic monks and lay followers toward the new light of realization, urging them to step out of their previous understanding.

FEARLESSNESS, TRUST AND PERSISTENCE

The Buddha's lesson of fearlessness is rooted in being trustful and encountering reality with hope. The foundation of fearlessness lies in persistently facing challenges with a spirit of never giving up. The Buddha's persistence until attaining Nirvana serves as an example. His final message to disciples emphasized the importance of persistence in seeking self-enlightenment. To fully embrace higher truths, individuals must liberate themselves from previous knowledge, let go and be open to transformation. This process requires guts and goes beyond mere intellectual reasoning or philosophical jargon. Only by letting go of the old can one be ready for the new and discover the true self.

BUDDHA'S TEACHING ON ABSORPTION AND UTILIZATION

At the core of Buddhist teaching is the idea of absorbing and utilizing various aspects of life to realize truth. Whether one is a carpenter, business leader, inventor, or anyone else, there is no need to exclude professional life from spiritual practice. The key is to bring a meditative and mystical attitude and the courage to let go of tensions into any activity. Progress on the path, believing in the seed of Buddhahood within oneself is essential.

ENCOURAGEMENT TO EMBRACE BUDDHAHOOD WITHIN

The Buddha consistently encouraged and emboldened people by asserting that the seed of Buddhahood resides within them. This concept, recognizing infinity within oneself, is empowering. In Japan, China, and other regions where Buddhism spread, it became a way of life, transforming ordinary activities into meditative practices. Whether a farmer, laborer, or any other profession, individuals could integrate different life energies with the mystical search.

TRANSCENDING FEAR AND EMBRACING CONSCIOUS CHOICE

Bring the Bodhisattva's action into everyday life, the Buddha emphasized transcending fear, be it fear of God, heaven, or hell. Buddha urged people to continue serving and fulfilling their roles while never forgetting the essential mystical search. The circumstances of life are coincidental, but the conscious choice lies in fixing the mind to bring greater awareness to thoughts and actions courageously and boldly.

MEDITATIVE QUALITY IN ORDINARY ACTIONS

Buddhism teaches that even in ordinary actions, such as breathing, one can bring forth the quality of Buddhahood. The breathing meditation, a practice employed by the Buddha, exemplifies how individuals can infuse a meditative quality even in the most straightforward acts. Observing the coming and going of breath allows the aspect of Buddhahood to shine through, transforming the ordinary into the extraordinary and fostering a sense of being that transcends the commonplace.

BUDDHISM: TRANSMUTATION OF THE ORDINARY INTO THE EXTRAORDINARY

At its essence, Buddhism is a transformative practice that aims to transmute the ordinary into the extraordinary. This transformation requires patience, perseverance, and a visionary commitment to a higher purpose. Actions are conducted not with worldly effort but with noble-heartedness fueled by a vision of something higher. Realizing this higher purpose brings true contentment, turning individuals into forces for good, not only within themselves but also for others.

ABUNDANT LIVING AND INNER RICHNESS:

In the Buddhist context, abundant living involves cultivating a sense of inner richness or abundance and channeling that abundance into creative and valuable contributions to the world. This abundance is not confined to material wealth but extends to meaningful passion, action, and a sense of purpose. The key is integrating spirituality into day-to-day actions and thought processes, moving away from viewing it as a dreamy, mystical concept. In doing so, individuals realize that the inner shrine or temple exists within the heart.

INFINITE NATURE OF THE SELF

Intrinsic within every individual is the energy of the ocean, the galaxy's vibration, and the stars' light—all in miniature. The realization of one's infinite and unlimited nature is a central aspect of Buddhism. Bring a sense of unlimitedness into life, individuals are encouraged to tap into the inherent courage and boldness already present within them. This courageous approach catalyzes profound transformation and the realization of one's boundless potential.

CHAPTER 14

The Path of the Mystic Warrior

THE INNER WARRIOR'S PATH: EMBRACING COURAGE AND TRANQUILLITY IN BUDDHISM

In the realm of Buddhism, the true essence lies in cultivating an inner warriorhood—a courageous battle against internal adversaries such as anger, ego, despair, anxiety, and hopelessness. The victory over these inner struggles paves the way for triumph in the larger war of life itself. Surprisingly, the Buddha's message of peace paradoxically evolved into the ultimate warrior code in cultures like China and Japan.

The focus in Buddhism is on becoming a warrior within, eliminating inner aggressiveness and purifying one's energy. The Shaolin Temple in China, with its warrior-monks embodying Buddhist values through martial arts, exemplifies this fusion.

Similarly, the Samurai warriors in Japan emphasize that the essence lies in harnessing inner energy. Inspired by Buddhism, one key teaching in the way of the Samurai, the Bushido, is focussing on the *hara* or navel plexus. This is said to awaken great power, energy, strength, balance and courage, and is a key practise for Japanese martial artists (Aikido, Judo, Karate), meditators, theatre practitioners, etc.

The crux of Samurai philosophy involves attaining a calm focus of being, distilling and purifying the better self. The true spiritual warrior is one who conquers the inner battles, making the world of eternity and abundance accessible. The real richness of spirit is the blossoming of the inner flower, leading to spontaneous energy and the lighting of the lamp within oneself.

Becoming a warrior of the inner self facilitates an easier outward journey. The spiritual power and bravery acquired infuse actions in the external world easily, making even material pursuits seem effortless. "The Inner Warrior's Path" invites individuals to embark on a transformative journey, embracing courage and tranquility within, transcending into a realm of spiritual abundance and profound richness of spirit.

THE INVINCIBLE SPIRIT: UNLEASHING INNER WARRIORHOOD FOR A LIFE OF GRACE AND ABUNDANCE

Neglecting the spiritual power within oneself hinders the attainment of material power, as anxious and fearful energies block the path to true abundance. The profound message of the Buddha revolves around the transformation of one's being, delving deep into the subconscious fear through the practice of inner warriorhood.

The essence lies in being absorbed in the self, realizing that within lies the source of all. This transformation involves cultivating a calm and collected inner state, triggering energies to maximize life's goodness. Inner warriorhood is the key to unlocking happiness, grace, and beauty, infusing vigor and quality into every endeavor.

Across diverse Buddhist paths in Japan, China, South Korea, Vietnam, Sri Lanka, Myanmar, India, Tibet, or any school, the common thread is the sense of invincibility of the inner spirit. This invincibility, synonymous with the path of the Buddha, activates a true prayerfulness within, making all things possible. Life becomes an opportunity to be lived consciously, unbound by the known, and fearlessly venturing into the unknown—an embodiment of the true warrior spirit.

Examining the archetype of the Japanese Samurai or the warrior Arjuna in the Mahabharata, we discover that a genuine warrior first achieves victory in the inner spiritual state. The courage to face battles in material life stems from self-realization and the actualization of latent inner spiritual power. "The Invincible Spirit" beckons individuals to embark on a journey of inner transformation, unlocking the power within and navigating life's challenges with fearlessness and grace.

WARRIOR SPIRIT UNVEILED: CONQUERING FEAR TO IGNITE INNER COURAGE

The essence of the true warrior spirit lies in liberating the mind from the ceaseless loop of anxiety and inner turmoil, cutting at the roots of repressed fears. This transformative journey leads to a concentration and inner focus that transcends the feverish state of fear and anxiety—a formidable adversary within the human experience.

Buddhism tells us that, at its core, the most significant hindrance for individuals is the oppressive fear deep within, which limits dynamism and obstructs personal growth. It is a debilitating and irrelevant force in the human consciousness that can be eradicated like a warrior on a mission. Beyond this fear, a wellspring of courage resides within, constituting every individual's authentic and original face.

No external place of worship is needed. True warriorhood is about unlocking the doorways of one's individuality at the innermost center of being, allowing the consciousness of the higher self to manifest. The warrior's path involves creating a healthy awareness of the inner self, merging the dimensions of mind, body, and spirit to transform confusion and chaos into an energy of extraordinary clarity.

At a fundamental level, human confusion and mental turmoil impoverish spiritual well-being, making individuals weaker. Warriorhood, in its truest form, is a journey of inner strength—a process of fortifying oneself from within, transcending the chaos to emerge spiritually empowered and resilient. Embark on this transformative journey, conquering fear to ignite the inherent courage within.

BUDDHIST MYSTICISM: EMPOWERING THE INNER WARRIOR FOR FULFILLMENT IN LIFE

Contrary to appearances, Buddhist mysticism is a profound journey of empowerment. Monks, defenseless or powerless, are regarded as the most powerful because the mystical realms have been activated within them. The warrior of the inner domain taps into the highest energies, utilizing them to create value in the world. This, in turn, leads to a life of true fulfillment—a dance of joy and trust in the spectrum of life.

Success in every aspect, be it the respect from others or the opportunities life presents, becomes a manifestation of the joy of living. Trust in people, situations, and things deepens, allowing individuals to explore with great depth and richness. The true warrior ascends to the highest peaks of self, conquering the inner mountain of consciousness and experiencing blissfulness within.

The inner attitude becomes the key. Hope, vigor, strength, and determination pave the way for outer accomplishments. In various human pursuits—academics, business, sports, art, and science—the essence lies in persistence and surpassing limitations. While physical limitations exist, the domain of consciousness is boundless, emphasizing the warrior's journey into this realm.

The realization dawns that the greatest skill lies in being peaceful and silent within, concentrating energy. As this inner transformation occurs, life's obstacles dissolve, enabling the integrated utilization of energy. "Buddhist Mysticism" invites individuals on a transformative journey, empowering the inner warrior to climb the highest peaks of self and create a harmonious and fulfilled life.

THE MYSTIC WARRIOR'S PATH: INTEGRATING ENERGIES FOR HARMONY AND TRANSCENDENCE

In pursuing inner warriorhood, the essence lies in integrating the energies of mind, body, and spirit, achieving a profound harmony of being. Drawing parallels from scientific principles and the yin-yang philosophy in China, the inner warrior unifies the dual aspects of us, creating a oneness within.

The mind, often divided into left and right hemispheres, is harmonized at a deeply meditative level. Warriorhood is about transcending wasteful psychic energy spent on countless thoughts leading to mental and emotional turmoil. Instead of escaping circumstances or anxiety, the warrior faces them, transcending and harmonizing dimensions of energy without force or mechanical effort.

The teachings of Buddha emphasize the transcendence of suffering, urging individuals to become multidimensional inner warriors unafraid of their simplicity and purity of consciousness. Therapy lies in setting aside thoughts, detaching from their influence, and seeing oneself as one truly is. This fundamental aspect of Buddhism involves therapeutic practices and the art of meditation as taught by Buddha, allowing individuals to function from their intuitive and higher selves.

The mystic warrior, characterized by intuitive energy, encourages individuals to become their intuitive warriors, tapping into the infinite possibilities, optimum functioning, and richness of the universe with each moment. Meet life's challenges in the spirit of the inner warrior, realizing that infinity and universal richness are available to those who embrace their intuitive selves.

CHAPTER 15

The Courage to Walk on Buddha's Path

IGNITING THE SPIRITUAL FLAME: THE ART OF MYSTICAL EXPLORATION

Embarking on Buddha's mystical path requires profound courage and passion. According to Buddha, only a rare few possess the genuine interest and longing, or *'apekkha,'* for spiritual salvation.

The initial step, driven by a thirst for mystical and spiritual inquiries, sets the transformative journey toward super-consciousness in motion, transcending ordinary limitations and unlocking infinite potential.

Deep within each of us lies an unexplored treasure, yet only a courageous few are willing to embark on the quest to unveil it. The mystical journey is akin to a treasure hunt, demanding a restless spirit to initiate the walk—a readiness and eagerness to venture into the uncharted realms of self-discovery.

THE INNER PILGRIMAGE: UNVEILING TRANQUILITY THROUGH MYSTICAL ANSWERS

Embarking on the journey toward tranquility involves seeking mystical answers to life's quandaries and profound questions. While mysticism is sometimes associated with religion in a conventional sense, its true essence, as emphasized by the Buddha's pursuit of the circle of dharma, lies in an extraordinary and esoteric exploration—a deep-rooted inner pilgrimage.

This inner journey brings one face-to-face with life's paramount aspects, unraveling answers to long-held questions. With each revelation, a sense of satisfaction and fulfillment emerges, giving rise to love and an impassioned pursuit of goodness. The accumulation of inner energy becomes a transformative force, enabling individuals to contribute significantly to the world.

The challenge for many lies in the outward orientation of their goals, while the mystical quest emphasizes an inward trajectory. The real direction, as Buddhism teaches, is to find the center of oneself—an inner summit and true treasure, often referred to as the diamond within. This ongoing quest is far from mundane; instead, it evokes spiritual bliss, passion, and enthrallment, encouraging individuals to explore new understanding territories and enter an exciting phase of life. By discovering significance within, one naturally becomes more alert and capable in the outer world, breaking free from mechanical patterns.

SPONTANEITY OF BEING: THE MYSTICAL QUEST FOR CONSCIOUS LIVING

The external mechanics of human existence often lead to habitual and mechanical patterns. Breaking free from this requires recognizing the divine element within oneself. The essence of the mystical search revolves around seeking the 'beloved' of the heart with passion and longing. This ultimate beloved, hidden deep within, is the profound inner treasure.

In this journey, the belief that every inner need will find fulfillment is paramount. The mystical quest transcends conventional notions of success or reaching specific goals. Every step and moment on this path hold meaning, bringing individuals closer to their self-truth and the truth of existence.

Spirituality is about navigating life with the utmost consciousness. A spontaneous sense of realizing one's foundational energy is crucial to achieve this. Discovering these foundations brings delight and a renewed sense of childhood, akin to the mystical seeker's comparison to a child. The emergence of energy within leads to personal fulfillment and catalyzes and energizes actions in the world.

The mystical passion awakened by this journey transforms individuals, making them single-minded, committed and passionate. It opens doors to new dimensions, both material and spiritual, fostering patience, trust, and a broader perspective on life. This shift allows an escape from the confines of narrow desires, embracing a richer, more profound experience of existence.

TRANSCENDING THE ORDINARY: THE ALCHEMY OF SPIRITUAL PASSION

Life possesses an inherent beauty that surpasses our perception, waiting to be seen in a more poetic and colorful light. This shift requires a profound longing for the extraordinary, a yearning for the sublime. Spiritual passion is the catalyst that dissolves individual existence into the greater, resulting in an elevation in every aspect of life.

Engaging in a genuine mystical quest brings a transformative experience, where joy becomes so abundant that energies are dynamically shared with others. Unnecessary burdens are shed, discontentment transforms into fulfillment, and a rush of awareness effortlessly brings happiness.

True self-prestige and confidence emerge, surpassing the superficial markers of outward respectability.

This mystical journey unveils the subtlety of joy, inviting an exploration of joyful energy present in all aspects of life. Nature, relationships, and work are seen differently, transcending conventional religious language and embracing passionate longing. Beyond words, this quest delves into the domain of being, where alchemy occurs, turning the ordinary into the extraordinary. Mundane experiences become extraordinary, consciousness evolves into super-consciousness, and human abilities transcend into superhuman capabilities. The essence of Buddha's teachings lies in this alchemy—a religion without religion, a passionate journey toward the extraordinary.

THE ART OF MYSTICISM: UNEARTHING INNER TREASURES FOR ULTIMATE FULFILLMENT

Discovering the greatest part of oneself is an art mastered through mysticism—a journey into a dimension of fulfillment that transcends material pursuits. The irony of life lies in the realization that what one thought would bring fulfillment often falls short, while small and insignificant aspects harbor the deepest treasures. The key lies in becoming a passionate treasure hunter of the self, delving into the inner spirit to unveil the ultimate achievements within one's consciousness.

In the mystical journey, the materialization of inner treasures becomes the primary quest. It involves exercising one's entire being—knowledge, experience, and energy—in a passionate pursuit of self-discovery. Digging deep within, the radiant treasure of the spirit awaits, ready to be uncovered. The process leads to a natural by-product of bliss, joy, fulfillment, courage, and grace. The seeker transforms into a seer of truth, progressing toward enlightenment as boundaries dissolve.

The inner world experiences a profound shift—greater joy, increased fulfillment, enhanced integratedness, and peace. The mind's incessant chatter evolves into a tranquil silence, allowing the individual to embody the ideals found in spiritual scriptures and mystical traditions. The mystical journey is a transformative odyssey that leads to self-realization and the discovery of a profound inner silence, bringing one closer to the essence of spirituality and enlightenment.

UNLOCKING THE MYSTICAL EXPERIENCE: EMBRACING THE PATH TO ENLIGHTENMENT

Gautam Buddha asserted that the profound experience of the enlightened ones is within our reach. The mystical path holds the magic that allows us to encounter the same states of being that Buddha himself experienced. He emphasized that everyone is special and can tap into the treasures within. The levels of cosmic being and the pure space of enlightenment that Buddha explored are accessible to us as well.

Buddha's message is clear: a little courage is needed to realize that beneath the surface of misery lies our inherent joy, bliss, and enlightenment. By initiating the journey with thirst, courage, and passion, we can awaken these dormant aspects of ourselves. As we traverse the path, we recognize the apex within—the summit of all spiritual possibilities. This awareness brings joy and instills a profound sense of capability.

Walking the mystical path clears the mental clutter, eliminates unnecessary limitations, and provides clarity. It transforms us into insiders of truth, enabling us to decipher the reality of life. With this newfound power of mind and spirit, we find more joy in our work and experience a deep sense of rejoicing in life. In this sense, true spirituality is not merely about God; it is about creating an inner environment that opens the door to fresh dimensions of life and living.

The journey begins with a longing, a thirst, and a passionately courageous commitment to walking the mystical path. This path is key to unlocking the mysteries within and leads us to the essence of true spirituality—joy, fulfillment, and a profound understanding of life.

UNVEILING INNER FORTITUDE: THE FIVE POWERS OF GENUINE COURAGE IN BUDDHISM

Embark on a journey into the heart of authentic spirituality as illuminated by Buddhism, where the inherent powers within us, known as Bala in Pali, take center stage.

Delve into the essence of five pivotal powers—faith, energy, mindfulness (*Sati*), concentration (*Samadhi*), and wisdom (*Panna/Prajna*)—each celebrated for its transformative significance. Discover the unwavering strength of these powers as they stand firm against adversities: faith counters doubt, energy battles lethargy, mindfulness triumphs over forgetfulness, concentration subdues distractions, and wisdom dispels ignorance.

By cultivating correct intentions, fostering mindfulness, embracing meditation, and exerting diligent effort, we nurture the growth of these powers within ourselves, paving the path toward spontaneous courage and unwavering fearlessness in our daily lives.

CHAPTER 16

Fearless Living: Lessons from Buddhist Philosophy

Buddhism has several secrets and key teachings that make us far more capable of living courageously and dynamically. These are called the wholesome or *Kushala* factors. Amongst these are the *Sobhana Chitta*, *Sobhana sadharana*, and the splendid consciousness factors. These are:

1. Confidence and faith which in Pali is called *Saddha*.

2. Mindfulness which in Pali is called *Sati*.

3. Decency which in Pali is called *Hiri*.

4. Modesty which in Pali is called *Ottappa*.

5. Lack of hatred which in Pali is called *Adosha*.

6. Lack of greed, which in Pali is called *Alobha*.

7. Equanimity which in Pali is called *Tatramajjhatata*.

8. Calmness of thoughts which in Pali is called *Kayapassadhi*.

9. Calmness of consciousness which in Pali is called *Chittapassadhi*.

10. Lightness of thoughts which in Pali is called *Kayalahuta*.

11. Lightness of consciousness which in Pali is called *Chittalahuta*.

12. Adaptability of thoughts and the mental body which in Pali is called *Kayamuduta*.

13. Adaptability of consciousness which in Pali is called *Chittamuduta*.

14. Adaptability of thoughts and the mental body which in Pali is called *Kayakamanatta*.

15. Adaptability of consciousness which in Pali is called *Chittakammanata*.

16. Excellence of thoughts which in Pali is called *Kayapagunattha*.

17. Excellence of consciousness which in Pali is called *Chittapagunnata*.

18. Uprighteousness of thoughts which in Pali is called *Kayujukata*.

19. Uprighteousness of consciousness which in Pali is called *Chittujukata*.

Moreover, Buddhism teaches us that there are five aids to enlightenment and dynamic living. These are:

1. Faith or *shraddha*, called *dad pa* in Tibetan.

2. Patient effort or *virya*, called *brtson 'grus* in Tibetan.

3. Mindfulness or *smriti*, called *dran pa* in Tibetan.

4. Concentration or *samadhi*, called *ting nge 'dzin* in Tibetan.

5. Wisdom or *prajñā*, called *shes rab* in Tibetan.

Furthermore, Buddhism teaches us to abstain from three kinds of conduct:

1. Abstinence from physical misconduct, known as *Kayaduccharita Virati* in Pali.

2. Refraining from verbal misconduct, termed *Vachiduccharita Virati* in the Buddha's Pali.

3. Avoiding mental misconduct, referred to as *Manoduccharita Virati* in the Buddha's Pali.

We must avoid these behaviors and instead cultivate compassion (*Karuna*), empathetic joy (*Mudita*), and wisdom (*Panya*).

By doing so, we distance ourselves from the fourteen *Akushala* or unwholesome mental factors described in Buddhist scriptures:

1. Delusion (*Moha*)
2. Lack of decency (*Ahirika*)
3. Lack of modesty (*Anottappa*)
4. Restlessness (*Uddhacca*)
5. Wrong views (*Ditthi*)
6. Greed (*Lobha*)
7. Hatred (*Dosa*)
8. Conceit (*Mana*)
9. Stinginess (*Maccharya*)
10. Jealousy (*Issa*)
11. Laziness (*Thina*)
12. Remorse (*Kukkucca*)
13. Apathy (*Middha*)

14. Doubt, skepticism, and over-skepticism, collectively known as *Vichikiccha*.

By eschewing these attitudes, we progress toward enlightenment, *Nirvana*, or *Nibbanna*, and embrace a bold and daring approach to life.

To swiftly move toward a courageous, noble, and adventurous state of being, Buddhism teaches us the ten recollections, also known as the ten contemplations or recollections, called *anusmriti*, and in Tibetan Buddhism, *rjes su dran pa*. These meditations or contemplations include:

1. Reflecting on the Buddha
2. Contemplating the Dharma
3. Meditating on morality
4. Reflecting on the Sangha or community
5. Recognizing true monks and renunciates within Buddhism
6. Embracing renunciation and cultivating a generous spirit
7. Reflecting on divine entities
8. Practicing breath meditation, known as *Anapana*, and in Tibetan *dbugs phyi nang du rgyu ba rjes su dran pa*

9. Contemplating unsavory aspects of existence, known as *Udvega*, to transcend mental conditioning
10. Reflecting on death, known as *Marana*, to overcome the fear of death
11. Meditating on the body, known as *Kayagata*, to overcome bodily fears

These practices collectively lead us toward the five powers in Buddhism, which empower us to transcend fear and live courageously. These powers are:

1. The power of faith, known as *Shraddha Bala*
2. The power of effort, known as *Virya Bala*
3. The power of mindfulness, known as *Smriti Bala*
4. The power of concentration, known as *Samadhi Bala*
5. The power of wisdom, known as *Pragya Bala*

Through such contemplation and meditations, we attain the seven riches of life, which are:

1. Confidence in faith, called *Shraddha*
2. Vigorous effort, or *Virya*
3. Moral living, or *Shila*

4. Decency, or *Apatrapya*
5. Learning, or *Shruta*
6. Renunciation, or *Prahana* (through suppressing negative emotions), or *Tyaga*
7. True wisdom, called *Pragya*

By cultivating these qualities, we become capable of following the path of the Buddhas and imbibing their strength. The path of the Buddhas and the Bodhisattvas makes us courageous, as well as:

1. Joyful
2. Near perfect
3. Radiant
4. Strong
5. Luminous
6. Still and steadfast
7. Of auspicious intellect
8. Truly worthy of the Buddha's Dharma.

All appearances are fog-like, mist-like!
Milarepa

*To become a Buddha, throw life's
common goals to the wind!*
Milarepa

OM MANI PADME HUM

Acknowledgments

I would like to express my sincere gratitude to the individuals who have played a pivotal role in bringing this series to life: Anuj Bahri, my exceptional literary agent at Red Ink; Gaurav Sabharwal and Shantanu Duttagupta, my outstanding publishers at Fingerprint! Publishing, along with their dedicated team. Special thanks to Shilpa Mohan, my editor for her invaluable contributions.

I would also like to extend my heartfelt appreciation to my parents, Anita and Captain Jeet Gupta, for their unwavering support throughout this journey. To my beloved sister, Priti and brother-in-law, Manish Goel, thank you for always being there for me. My niece, Vaanee and nephew, Kartikay, have been a constant source of joy and inspiration and I am grateful for their presence in my life.

I am truly humbled by the collective efforts and encouragement from all these remarkable individuals, without whom this series would not have been possible.

Pranay is a renowned mystic, captivating speaker and accomplished author who has dedicated his life to exploring the depths of spirituality. With a deep understanding of the human experience and an unwavering commitment to personal growth, Pranay has written numerous books that offer insights into the realms of spirituality.

One of Pranay's most celebrated contributions is his groundbreaking series of modules titled "Advanced Spirituality for Leadership and Success." His transformative PowerTalks and MysticTalks have garnered international recognition for their exceptional ability to inspire and empower individuals from all walks of life. Pranay's unique approach combines ancient wisdom with contemporary insights, providing a roadmap for achieving spiritual fulfillment while embracing leadership qualities that lead to remarkable success.

To learn more about Pranay and his transformative teachings, visit his official website at pranay.org.

To buy more books by the author scan the QR code given below.